A Christmas Garland

This edition is published by Gramercy Books,
distributed by Random House Value Publishing, Inc.
40 Engelhard Avenue
Avenel, New Jersey 07001

Production supervised by Michael Siebert
Designed by Liz Trovato

Random House
New York • Toronto • London • Sydney • Auckland

Printed and bound in the United States of America

Library of Congress Cataloging–in–Publication Data
A christmas garland.
p. cm.
ISBN 0–517–14738–6
1. Christmas—Literary collections. I. Hudson, Grace.
II. Tarrant, Margaret, 1888–1959.
PN6071.C6C525
808.81'933—dc20   95–17658
                                                  CIP

8 7 6 5 4 3 2 1

A CHRISTMAS GARLAND

Stories, poems, and prayers for the holiday season

Illustrated by Margaret Tarrant
Compiled by Grace Hudson

GRAMERCY BOOKS
New York • Avenel

Contents

8.99

Margaret W. Tarrant

Introduction

Christmas has become a wonderful amalgam of customs and traditions. It is a special and joyous season when friends and families gather to exchange gifts, to eat together, and to express warm and generous feelings.

All too often, however, people forget that Christmas is also a time of reflection and renewal, a time not only to sing carols, but to listen, really listen, to the words. It is a time, too, to read aloud and to share some of the season's great prayers and poems, as well as the traditional stories. For Christmas is a glorious birthday party, a celebration of the birth of Jesus Christ.

A Christmas Garland is a fine collection of readings to be enjoyed by the whole family during this joyous season. The charming illustrations by the well-known English artist Margaret W. Tarrant, and Liz Trovato's lovely design, make this a book which will be treasured for many years to come.

And there were in the same country
shepherds abiding in the field, keeping watch
over their flock by night.

And, lo, the angel of the Lord came upon
them, and the glory of the Lord shone round
about them; and they were sore afraid.

And the angel said unto them, Fear not:
for behold, I bring you good tidings of great
joy, which shall be to all people.

For unto you is born this day,
in the city of David, a Savior, which is
Christ the Lord.

And this shall be a sign unto you;
Ye shall find the babe wrapped in swaddling
clothes, lying in a manger.

And suddenly there was with the angel
a multitude of the heavenly host
praising God, and saying,

Glory to God in the highest, and on earth
peace, good will toward men.

And it came to pass,
as the angels were gone away from
them into heaven, the shepherds said one to
another, Let us now go even unto Bethlehem,
and see this thing which is come to pass,
which the Lord hath made known unto us.

And they came with haste,
and found Mary and Joseph, and the babe
lying in a manger.

SAINT LUKE

Real Christmas

I n a western town where the old mission spirit still lives, the people celebrate Christmas by going to church. On Christmas Eve the altar is dressed with candles and close by, the scene of the nativity is laid reverently. The holy child lies in the manger, his mother kneeling on one side, his father on the other. At his feet stand the three wise men bringing gifts. The animals kneel in their stalls, all but the little donkey who peers down into the face of the sleeping child. A group of shepherds listens to the angel choir and a bright star shines down. The scene gives a feeling of sanctity. It is very lovely.

Early Christmas morning, before anyone else would be likely to be out, the old priest went to his church to see that all was as it should be for the first service. He was horrified to discover the manger empty and the Christ Child gone. After an unbelieving glance around the church, he rushed out into the street.

No one was there except a tiny boy who pulled a

little red wagon behind him. He walked slowly, solemnly toward the church and the priest was almost on top of him before he noticed him. Imagine his amazement when he saw the missing Christ Child, carefully wrapped in a scarlet sweater, lying in the little wagon.

"What, what's this? How——" But all dread and anger fled from the good man's heart as he looked into the innocent face before him. He saw that whatever had been done was done for goodness' sake.

"Tell me why you did this, my son."

"Because, Father, I prayed for a red wagon for Christmas and I promised that if I got it, I would give the Little Lord Jesus the first ride. So I did. Now I'm going to take him back to his mother and say a prayer of thanks."

"We will go together," said the priest and, hand in hand, the old, old man and the very small boy went into the church carrying the holy child.

ANGELO PATRI

The Crèche

Come, hang the greens and plant the tree,
    And light the Christmas candles;
Your carols sing of wise men three,
    Of shepherds in their sandals.

Go get you straw and get you wood
    And build again the stable,
For you will find it very good
    Who dress in silk and sable.

Go build again the wooden bed,
    The cattle standing round it,
The straw to pillow His sweet head,
    The shepherds to surround it.

Then kneel beside the manger bed,
    And feel the loving awe
That takes all simple-hearted folk
    Who kneel upon the straw.

ALICE GREGG

Little Lamb, Who Made Thee?

Little lamb, who made thee?

Dost thou know who made thee,

Gave thee life, and bid thee feed

By the stream and o'er the mead;

Gave thee clothing of delight,

Softest clothing, woolly, bright;

Gave thee such a tender voice,

Making all the vales rejoice?

Little Lamb, who made thee?

Dost thou know who made thee?

Little lamb, I'll tell thee;

Little lamb, I'll tell thee;

He is called by thy name,

For He calls Himself a Lamb.

He is meek, and He is mild,

He became a little child,

I a child, and thou a lamb,

We are called by His name.

Little lamb, God bless thee!

Little lamb, God bless thee!

WILLIAM BLAKE

A Little Child

A little child,
   A shining star.
A stable rude,
   The door ajar.

Yet in that place,
   So crude, forlorn,
The Hope of all
   The world was born.

AUTHOR UNKNOWN

The Angel's Story

Through the blue and frosty heavens
  Christmas stars were shining bright;
Glistening lamps throughout the city
  Almost matched their gleaming light;
While the winter snow was lying,
And the winter winds were sighing,
  Long ago, one Christmas night.

While from every tower and steeple
  Pealing bells were sounding clear,
(Never were such tones of gladness
  Save when Christmas time is near),
Many a one that night was merry
  Who had toiled through all the year.

That night saw old wrongs forgiven,
    Friends, long parted, reconciled;
Voices all unused to laughter,
    Mournful eyes that rarely smiled,
Trembling hearts that feared the morrow,
    From their anxious thoughts beguiled.

Rich and poor felt love and blessing
    From the gracious season fall;
Joy and plenty in the cottage,
    Peace and feasting in the hall;
And the voices of the children
    Ringing clear above it all!

ADELAIDE ANNE PROCTER

The little maid
Could hear her lord
Shout at the bearded man
In the windy gloom:
"There is no room
Tonight in Bethl'hem khan."

The little maid
Unlatched the door
And snatched a hallway light:
"Oh, master, we can fix a bed
In the cave behind the inn," she said.
"By the manger where the calves are fed—
The lady can't ride on tonight."

All the night was leaping, leaping,
    Over old Judea's hills—
All the sheep were sleeping, sleeping,
    By the slowly purling rills.

All the stars were swinging, swinging,
    In the purple of the night—
Angels gathered, singing, singing,
    Then there was the Light.

C. F. B.

Love Among the Snows

Love awoke one winter's night
And wander'd through the snowbound land,
And calling to the beasts and birds
Bid them his message understand.

And from the forest all wild things
That crept or flew obeyed love's call,
And learned from him the golden words
Of brotherhood for one and all.

AUTHOR UNKNOWN

Christmas Bells

I heard the bells on Christmas Day
Their old familiar carols play,
And wild and sweet
The word repeat
Of peace on earth, good will to men!

And thought how, as the day had come,
The belfries of all Christendom
Had rolled along
The unbroken song
Of peace on earth, good will to men!

Till, ringing, swinging on its way,
The world revolved from night to day
A voice, a chime,
A chant sublime
Of peace on earth, good will to men!

Then from each black, accursed mouth
The cannon thundered in the South

And with the sound
The carols drowned
Of peace on earth, good will to men!

It was as if an earthquake rent
The hearthstones of a continent,
And made forlorn
The households born
Of peace on earth, good will to men!

And in despair I bowed my head;
"There is no peace on earth," I said;
"For hate is strong
And mocks the song
Of peace on earth, good will to men!"
Then pealed the bells more loud and deep,
"God is not dead; nor doth He sleep!
The Wrong shall fail,
The Right prevail,
With peace on earth, good will to men!"

HENRY WADSWORTH LONGFELLOW

Babushka
A Russian Legend

Babushka sits before the fire
    Upon a winter's night;
The driving winds heap up the snow,
    Her hut is snug and tight;
The howling winds—they only make
    Babushka's fire more bright!

She hears a knocking at the door:
    So late—who can it be?
She hastes to lift the wooden latch,
    No thought of fear has she;
The wind-blown candle in her hand
    Shines out on strangers three.

Their beards are white with age, and snow
    That in the darkness flies;
Their floating locks are long and white,
    But kindly are their eyes
That sparkle underneath their brows,
    Like stars in frosty skies.

"Babushka, we have come from far,
　　We tarry but to say,
A little Prince is born this night,
　　Who all the world shall sway.
Come join the search, go with us,
　　We go our gifts to pay."

Babushka shivers at the door;
　　"I would I might behold
The little Prince who shall be King
　　But ah! the night is cold,
The wind so fierce, the snow so deep,
　　And I, good sirs, am old."
The strangers three, no word they speak,
　　But fade in snowy space!
Babushka sits before her fire,
　　And dreams, with wistful face:
"I would that I had questioned them,
　　So I the way might trace!"

"When morning comes with blessed light,
　　I'll early be awake:

My staff in hand I'll go—perchance,
  Those strangers I'll o'ertake;
And, for the Child some little toys
  I'll carry, for His sake.''

The morning came, and staff in hand,
  She wandered in the snow,
She asked the way of all she met,
  But none the way could show.
''It must be farther yet,'' she sighed:
  ''Then farther will I go.''

And still, 'tis said, on Christmas Eve,
  When high the drifts are piled,
With staff, with basket on her arm,
  Babushka seeks the Child:
At every door her face is seen,
  Her wistful face and mild!

Her gifts at every door she leaves:
  She bends and murmurs low,
Above each little face half-hid

By pillows white as snow:
"And is He here?" Then, softly sighs,
"Nay, farther must I go!"

EDITH M. THOMAS

While Shepherds
Watched Their Flocks

While shepherds watched their flocks
by night,
All seated on the ground,
The angel of the Lord came down,
And glory shone around,
And glory shone around.

"Fear not!" said He, for mighty dread
Had seized their troubled mind,
"Glad tidings of great joy I bring,
To you and all mankind,
To you and all mankind,

"To you, in David's town, this day
Is born of David's line

30

The Savior who is Christ the Lord,
  And this shall be the sign,
    And this shall be the sign.''

''The Heav'nly Babe you there shall find
  To human view displayed,
All meanly wrapped in swathing band
  And in a manger laid,
    And in a manger laid.''

''All glory be to God on high,
  And to the earth be peace,
Good will henceforth from heav'n to men,
  Begin and never cease,
    Begin and never cease.''

NAHUM TATE

On Christmas Day

Darkness had fled away,
   Starlight had led the way,
Love shone as bright as day,
   Where Jesus lay.

He was so dear and small,
   Not like a king at all,
Wrapped in His mother's shawl,
   Cradled in hay.

Stars in His mother's eyes
   Leaned down from Paradise,
Crowned God in humble guise
   Where Jesus lay.

Softly the beasts gave tongue,
   What songs they knew, they sung,
Sweetly the stable rung
   Where Jesus lay.

Lift now your voice and sing,
   Letting your carols ring
For Jesus Christ your king
   On Christmas Day.

ELSIE WILLIAMS CHANDLER

Child Jesus

When the Christ Child to this world came down,
He left for us his throne and crown,
He lay in a manger, all pure and fair,
Of straw and hay His bed so bare.
But high in heaven the star shone bright,
And the oxen watched by the babe that night.
    Hallelujah! Child Jesus!

Oh, come, ye sinful and ye who mourn,
Forgetting all your sin and sadness,
In the city of David a child is born,
Who doth bring us heav'nly gladness.
Then let us to the manger go,
To seek the Christ who hath loved us so.
    Hallelujah! Child Jesus!

HANS CHRISTIAN ANDERSEN

Where Is the Babe?

Tell us, thou clear and heavenly tongue,
Where is the babe but lately sprung,
Lies he the lily banks among?

Or say if this new birth of ours
Sleeps, laid within some ark of flowers,
Spangled with dew-light; thou canst clear
All doubts, and manifest the where.

Declare to us bright star, if we shall seek
Him in the morning's blushing cheek,
Or search the beds of spices through,
To find him out?

ROBERT HERRICK

The Friendly Beasts

Jesus our brother, strong and good,
Was humbly born in a stable rude,
And the friendly beasts around Him stood,
Jesus our brother, strong and good.

"I," said the donkey, shaggy and brown,
"I carried His Mother up hill and down,
I carried her safely to Bethlehem town;
I," said the donkey, shaggy and brown.

"I," said the cow, all white and red,
"I gave Him my manger for His bed."
"I," said the sheep with curly horn,
"I gave Him my wool for His blanket warm."

And every beast, by some good spell,
In the stable dark was glad to tell,
Of the gift he gave Immanuel,
The gift he gave Immanuel.

A TWELFTH-CENTURY CAROL

The Legend of Saint Nicholas

Once upon a time there lived in Myra a good man named Nicholas. When he was a young man his father and mother died of the plague, and he was left the sole heir of all their vast estate. But he looked upon all this money as belonging to God and felt that he, himself, was merely the steward of God's mercies. So he went about everywhere doing good and sharing his riches with all those who were in need.

Now, there lived in that country a certain nobleman who had three beautiful daughters. He had been very rich, but he lost all his property and became so poor that he did not know what to do to provide for his family. His daughters were anxious to be married, but their father had no money to give them dowries and, in that country, no maiden could marry unless she had her marriage portion, or dowry. They were so very poor that they had scarcely enough food to eat. Their clothes were so worn and ragged that they would not go out of the house and their father was overcome with shame and sorrow.

When the good Nicholas heard of their troubles he longed to help them. He knew that the father was proud and that it would be hard to give him money; so he thought that it would be best to surprise them with a gift. Then Nicholas took some gold and, tying it in a long silken purse, went at once to the home of the poor nobleman. It was night and the beautiful maidens were fast asleep while the broken-hearted father, too wretched to go to bed, sat by the fireside watching and praying.

Nicholas stood outside, wondering how he could bestow his gift without being seen, when suddenly the moon came from behind the clouds and he saw that a window in the house was open. Creeping softly to the open window, he threw the purse right into the room where it fell at the feet of the nobleman. The father picked up the purse and was very surprised to find it full of gold pieces.

Awakening his daughters the father said, ''See this purse which came through the window and fell at my feet. It is indeed a gift from Heaven. God has remembered us in our time of need.''

After they had rejoiced together, they agreed to give most of the gold to the eldest daughter, so that she would have her dowry and could wed the young man she loved.

Not long after that, Nicholas filled another silken purse with gold and again he went by night so that no one should see him, and he threw this purse, too, through the open window. When the father saw this

golden gift he again gave thanks. The money he gave to the second daughter who, like her sister, at once married the man of her choice.

Meanwhile the father was curious to find out who was so kind to them, for he wished to thank the person who had come in the night to help them with these golden gifts. So he watched and waited night after night. And after a time the good Nicholas came with another silken purse filled with gold pieces for the youngest daughter.

He was just about to throw it into the room when the nobleman rushed from the house and, seizing him by his long robe, knelt before him, saying, "Oh good Nicholas, servant of God, why seek to hide thyself?" And he kissed his hands and feet and tried to thank him.

But Nicholas answered, "Do not thank me, my good man, but thank the Heavenly Father who has sent me to you in answer to your prayers. I am only His messenger to help those who trust in Him. Tell no man of these gifts of gold, nor who brought them to you in the night, for my deeds are done in His name."

Thus the youngest daughter of the nobleman was married, and she and her father and sisters all lived happily the rest of their lives.

The good Nicholas went about from place to place,

and wherever he went he did deeds of kindness, so that all the people loved him.

One time he took a long journey to the Holy Land, and when he was upon the sea there came a terrible storm, so that the ship was tossed about and almost wrecked, and all the sailors gave up hope.

But the good Nicholas said, "Fear not, our Heavenly Father will bring us safely into harbor." Then he knelt and prayed to God and the storm ceased and the boat was brought safely to the land. Whereupon the sailors fell at the feet of Nicholas and thanked him.

He answered them humbly, "Thank your Father who is in Heaven, for He is the ruler of us all. It is He who rules the earth and the sky and the sea, and who, in His good mercy, spared our lives that we may serve Him."

When Nicholas returned from Palestine he went to the city of Myra, where he was appointed a bishop. After that he preached God's Word and went about doing good all of his life. When he died the people said, "We will not call him Bishop Nicholas, but we will call him Saint Nicholas, for if ever there was a saint upon earth it was our good Nicholas." And so to this day he is called Good Saint Nicholas.

And now in many countries they tell the story of the good Saint Nicholas, and how he goes about the

earth at Christmas time bringing gifts of love to all who deserve them, and, because he had put his gifts of gold in long silken purses, today children hang up their long stockings to hold his gifts. And when the children are very good he fills their stockings with sweets and toys and trinkets, but if they have been naughty, they will find a bunch of switches, showing that they deserve to be punished.

We all know that on Christmas Eve Saint Nicholas will come in the night, for he never likes to be seen. And we know that he will always live—for he is the spirit of love and love can never die.

So, every Christmas, let us give our gifts as he did those silken purses so long ago—without anyone knowing about it—and let our gifts be a surprise. Then we, too, can have the spirit of love and join in this celebration of Christmas with Good Saint Nicholas.

Georgene Faulkner

Away in a Manger

Away in a manger, no crib for a bed,
  The little Lord Jesus laid down his sweet head.
The stars in the sky looked down where he lay,
  The little Lord Jesus asleep in the hay.

The cattle are lowing, the baby awakes,
  But little Lord Jesus no crying he makes.
I love Thee, Lord Jesus, look down from the sky
  And stay by my side 'til morning is nigh.

Be near me, Lord Jesus, I ask Thee to stay
  Close by me forever, and love me, I pray.
Bless all the dear children in thy tender care,
  And fit us for heaven, to live with Thee there.

GERMAN CAROL

A Christmas Carol

In the bleak mid-winter
Frosty wind made moan,
Earth stood hard as iron,
Water like a stone;
Snow had fallen, snow on snow,
Snow on snow,
In the bleak mid-winter
Long ago.

Our God, Heaven cannot hold him
Nor earth sustain;
Heaven and earth shall flee away
When he comes to reign;
In the bleak mid-winter
A stable-place sufficed
The Lord God Almighty
Jesus Christ.

Angels and archangels
   May have gathered there,
Cherubim and seraphim
   Thronged the air;
But only His Mother
   In her maiden bliss
Worshipped the Beloved
   With a kiss.

What can I give Him,
   Poor as I am?
If I were a shepherd
   I would bring a lamb,
If I were a Wise Man
   I would do my part—
Yet what can I give Him,
   Give my heart.

CHRISTINA ROSSETTI

The First Supper

At the First Supper
  The guests were but one:
A maiden was the hostess,
  The guest her son.

At the First Supper
  No candles were lit:
In the darkness hay-scented
  They both did sit.

At the First Supper
  No table was spread:
In the curve of her elbow
  She laid his head.

At the First Supper
  They poured no wine:
On milk of the rarest
  The guest did dine.

She held him very closely
  Against her breast,
Her fair one, her dear one,
  Her darling guest;

She held him very closely,
    Guessing that this
Is the last that any mother
    May know of bliss.

JAN STRUTHER

A Prayer

Lord, make me a channel of Thy peace.

That where there is hatred I may bring love,
That where there is wrong I may bring the
    spirit of forgiveness,
That where there is discord I may bring harmony,
That where there is error I may bring truth,
That where there is doubt I may bring faith,
That where there is despair I may bring hope,
That where there are shadows I may bring
    Thy light,
That where there is sadness I may bring joy.

Lord, grant that I may seek rather
To comfort than to be comforted;
To understand than to be understood;
To love rather than to be loved.

For it is by giving that one receives;
It is by self-forgetting that one finds;
It is by forgiving that one is forgiven;
It is by dying—that one awakens to
    eternal life.

Little Jesus, wast Thou shy
Once, and just so small as I?
And what did it feel like to be
Out of Heaven, and just like me?
Didst thou sometimes think of *there*
And ask where all the angels were?
I should think that I would cry
For my house made all of sky;
I would look about the air,
And wonder where my angels were;
And at waking 'twould distress me—
Not an angel there to dress me!

FRANCIS THOMPSON

Christmas Music

While Mary sleeps the angels play
   A heavenly lullaby to soothe his infant sleep,
Singing their hymn of praise at close of day,
   While Joseph at the door his watch doth keep.

So, Father, at this Christmas may thy care
   Above the cradle of our little children ward;
Accepting, Lord, their infant thoughts as prayer,
   Bringing them daily nearer to their God.

AUTHOR UNKNOWN

Voices in the Mist

The time draws near the birth of Christ:
　　The moon is hid; the night is still;
The Christmas bells from hill to hill
　　Answer each other in the mist.

Four voices of four hamlets round,
　　From far and near, on mead and moor,
Swell out and fail, as if a door
　　Were shut between me and the sound:

Each voice four changes on the wind,
　　That now dilate, and now decrease,
Peace and goodwill, goodwill and peace,
　　Peace and goodwill, to all mankind.

ALFRED, LORD TENNYSON

Lo, in the Silent Night

Lo, in the silent night
  a child to God is born,
And all is brought again
  that ere was lost or lorn.
Could but thy soul, O man,
  become a silent night,
God would be born in thee,
  and set all things aright.

FIFTEENTH-CENTURY POEM

The Minstrels

The minstrels played their Christmas tune
   Tonight beneath my cottage eaves;
While, smitten by a lofty moon,
   The encircling laurels, thick with leaves,
Gave back a rich and dazzling sheen,
That overpowered their natural green.

Through hill and valley every breeze
   Had sunk to rest with folded wings
Keen was the air, but could not freeze,
   Nor check, the music of the strings;
So stout and hardy were the band
That scraped the chords with strenuous hand.

And who but listened—till was paid
   Respect to every inmate's claim,
The greeting given, the music played
   In honor of each household name,
Duly pronounced with lusty call,
And "Merry Christmas" wished to all.

WILLIAM WORDSWORTH

The Nativity

Thou cam'st from Heaven to earth, that we
Might go from earth to Heaven with Thee:
And though Thou found'st no welcome here,
Thou did'st provide us mansions there—
A stable was Thy court, and when
Men turn'd to beasts, beasts would be men:
They were Thy courtiers; others none;
And their poor manger was Thy Throne;
No swaddling silks Thy limbs did fold,
Though Thou could'st turn Thy rags to gold.
No rockers waited on Thy birth,
No cradles stirred, no songs of mirth;
But her chaste lap and sacred breast,
Which lodged Thee first, did give Thee rest.
But stay, what light is that doth stream
And drop here in a gilded beam,
It is Thy star runs page, and brings
Thy tributary Eastern Kings.
Lord! grant some light to us; that we
May with them find the way to Thee!
Behold what mists eclipse the day!
How dark it is! Shed down one ray,
To guide us out of this sad night,
And say once more,
"LET THERE BE LIGHT!"

HENRY VAUGHAN

58

Robin Redbreast

It happened at the time when our Lord created the world, when He not only made heaven and earth, but all the animals and the plants as well, at the same time giving them their names.

There have been many histories concerning that time, and if we knew them all, we should have light upon everything in this world which we can not now comprehend.

At that time it happened one day when our Lord sat in His Paradise and painted the little birds, that the colors in our Lord's paint pot gave out, and the goldfinch would have been without color if our Lord had not wiped all His paint brushes on its feathers.

It was then that the donkey got his long ears, because he could not remember the name that had been given him. No sooner had he taken a few steps over the meadows of Paradise than he forgot, and three times he came back to ask his name.

At last our Lord grew somewhat impatient, took him by his two ears, and said, "Thy name is ass, ass, ass!" And while He thus spake our Lord pulled both of his ears that the ass might hear better, and remember what was said to him.

It was on the same day, too, that the bee was punished. Now, when the bee was created, she began immediately to gather honey, and the animals and human beings who caught the delicious odor of the honey came and wanted to taste of it. But the bee wanted to keep it all for herself and with her poisonous sting pursued every living creature that approached her hive. Our Lord saw this, and at once called the bee to Him and punished her.

"I gave thee the gift of gathering honey, which is the sweetest thing in all creation," said our Lord, "but I did not give thee the right to be cruel to thy neighbor. Remember well that every time thou stingest any creature who desires to taste of thy honey, thou shalt surely die!"

Ah, yes! It was at that time, too, that the cricket became blind and the ant missed her wings. So many strange things happened on that day!

Our Lord sat there, big and gentle, and planned and created all day long, and toward evening He conceived the idea of making a little gray bird.

"Remember your name is Robin Redbreast," said our Lord to the bird, as soon as it was finished. Then He held it in the palm of His open hand and let it fly.

After the bird had been testing his wings a while, and had seen something of the beautiful world in which he was destined to live, he became curious to see what he himself was like. He noticed that he was

entirely gray, and that his breast was just as gray as all the rest of him. Robin Redbreast twisted and turned in all directions as he viewed himself in the mirror of a clear lake, but he couldn't find a single red feather. Then he flew back to our Lord.

Our Lord sat there on His throne, big and gentle. Out of His hands came butterflies that fluttered about His head; doves cooed on His shoulders; and out of the earth beneath Him grew the rose, the lily, and the daisy.

The little bird's heart beat heavily with fright, but with easy curves he flew nearer and nearer our Lord, until at last he rested on our Lord's hand. Then our Lord asked what the little bird wanted.

"I only wish to ask you about one thing," said the little bird.

"What is it you wish to know?" asked our Lord.

"Why should I be called Robin Redbreast, when I am all gray, from the tip of my bill to the very end of my tail? Why am I called Redbreast when I do not possess one single red feather?" The bird looked beseechingly on our Lord with his tiny black eyes—then turned his head. About him he saw pheasants all red under a sprinkle of gold dust, parrots with marvelous red neckbands, cocks with red combs, to say nothing about the butterflies, the goldfinches, and the roses!

And, naturally, he thought how little he needed—just one tiny drop of color on his breast and he, too, would be a beautiful bird, and his name would fit him. "Why should I be called Redbreast when I am so entirely gray?" asked the bird once again, and waited for our Lord to say: "Ah, my friend, I see that I have forgotten to paint your breast feathers red, but wait a moment and it shall be done."

But our Lord only smiled a little and said, "I have called you Robin Redbreast, and Robin Redbreast shall your name be, but you must look to it that you yourself earn your red breast feathers." Then our Lord lifted His hand and let the bird fly once more—out into the world.

The bird flew down into Paradise, meditating deeply.

What could a little bird like him do to earn for himself red feathers? The only thing he could think of was to make his nest in a brier bush. He built it in among the thorns in the close thicket. It looked as if he were waiting for a rose leaf to cling to his throat and give him color.

Countless years had come and gone since that day, which was the happiest in all the world! Human beings had already advanced so far that they had learned to

cultivate the earth and sail the seas. They had learned to make clothes and ornaments for themselves, and had long since learned to build big temples and great cities.

Then there dawned a new day, one that will long be remembered in the world's history. On the morning of this day Robin Redbreast sat upon a little naked hillock outside of Jerusalem's walls, and sang to his mate and his young ones, who rested in a small nest in a brier bush.

Robin Redbreast told the little ones all about that wonderful day of creation, and how the Lord had given names to everything, just as each Redbreast had told it ever since the first Redbreast had heard God's word, and gone out of God's hand. "And mark you," he ended sorrowfully, "so many years have gone, so many roses have bloomed, so many little birds have come out of their eggs since Creation Day, but Robin Redbreast is still a little gray bird that has not yet succeeded in gaining red feathers."

The little young ones opened wide their tiny bills, and asked if their forbears had never tried to do any great thing to earn the priceless red color.

"We have all done what we could," said the little bird, "but we have all gone amiss. Even the first Robin

Redbreast met one day another bird exactly like himself, just like your mother, and he began immediately to love it with such a mighty love that he could feel his breast burn. 'Ah!' he thought then, 'now I understand! It was our Lord's meaning that I should love with so much ardor that my breast should grow red in color from the very warmth of the love that lives in my heart.' But he missed it, as all those who came after him have missed it, and as even you shall miss it.''

The little young ones twittered, utterly bewildered, and already began to mourn because the red color would not come to beautify their little, downy gray breasts.

''We had also hoped that song would help us,'' said the grown-up bird, speaking in long, drawn-out tones. ''The first Robin Redbreast sang until his heart swelled within him, he was so carried away, and he dared to hope anew. 'Ah!' he thought, 'it is the glow of the song which lives in my soul that will color my breast feathers red.' But he missed it, as all the others have missed it and as even you shall miss it.'' Again was heard a sad ''peep'' from the young ones' half-naked throats.

''We had also counted on our courage and our valor,'' said the bird. ''The first Robin Redbreast fought bravely with other birds, until his breast flamed with the pride of conquest. 'Ah!' he thought, 'my breast feathers shall become red from the love of battle which burns in my heart.' He, too, missed it, as all those who came after him have missed it, and as even you shall miss it." The little young ones peeped courageously that they still wished to try and win the much desired prize, but the bird answered them sorrowfully that it would be impossible. What could they do when so many splendid ancestors had missed the mark? What could they do more than love, sing, and fight? What could—the little bird stopped short, for out of one of the gates of Jerusalem came a crowd of people marching, and the whole procession rushed toward the hillock, where the birds had their nest. Their were riders on proud horses, soldiers with long spears, executioners with nails and hammers. There were judges and priests in the procession, weeping women, and a mob of mad, loose people running about—a filthy, howling mob of loiterers.

The little gray bird sat trembling on the edge of his nest. He feared each instant that the little brier bush would be trampled down and his mate and his young ones killed!

"Be careful!" he cried to his mate and to the little defenseless young ones. "Stay close together and remain quiet. Here comes a horse that will ride right

67

over us! Here comes a warrior with iron-shod sandals! Here comes the whole wild, storming mob!'' Immediately the bird ceased his cry of warning and grew calm and quiet. He almost forgot the danger hovering over him. Finally, he hopped down into the nest and spread his wings over the young ones.

"Oh! This is too terrible," he said. "I don't wish you to witness this awful sight! There are three miscreants who are going to be crucified!" And he spread his wings so the little ones could see nothing.

They caught only the sound of hammers, the cries of anguish, and the wild shrieks of the mob.

Robin Redbreast followed the whole spectacle with his eyes, which grew big with terror. He could not take his glance from the three unfortunates.

"How terrible human beings are!" said the bird after a little while. "It isn't enough that they nail these poor creatures to a cross, but they even place a crown of piercing thorns upon the head of one of them. I see that the thorns have wounded his brow so that the blood flows," he continued. "And this man is so beautiful, and looks about him with such mild glances that everyone ought to love him. I feel as if an arrow were shooting through my heart when I see him suffer!"

The little bird began to feel a stronger and stronger pity for the thorn-crowned sufferer. Oh! If I were only my brother the eagle, he thought, I would draw the nails from his hands, and with my strong claws I would drive away all those who torture him! He saw how the blood trickled down from the brow of the Crucified One, and he could no longer remain quiet in his nest. Even if I am little and weak, I can still do something for this poor tortured man, thought the bird. Then he left his nest and flew out into the air, striking wide circles around the Crucified One. He flew around him several times without daring to approach, for he was a shy little bird, who had never dared to go near a human being. But little by little he gained courage, flew close to him, and with his little bill drew out a thorn that had become imbedded in his brow. And as he did this there fell on his breast a drop of blood from the face of the Crucified One. It spread quickly and floated out and colored all of the bird's fine little breast feathers.

Then the Crucified One opened his lips and whispered to the bird, "Because of thy compassion, thou hast won all that thy kind have been striving after, ever since the world was created."

As soon as the bird had returned to his nest, his young ones cried to him, "Thy breast is red! Thy breast feathers are redder than the roses!"

"It is only a drop of blood from the poor man's

forehead," said the bird. "It will vanish as soon as I bathe in a pool or a clear well."

But no matter how much the little bird bathed, the red color did not vanish—and when the little young ones grew up, the blood-red color shone on their breast feathers, too, just as it shines on every Robin Redbreast's throat and breast until this very day.

SELMA LAGERLÖF

Christmas Joys

Let us honor, O my brothers,
  Christmas Day!
Call a truce then
  to our labors,
Let us feast with
  friends and neighbors
And be merry as the custom of
  our caste.

RUDYARD KIPLING

God Bless the Little Things

God bless the little things this Christmastide,
All the little wild things that live outside;
Little cold robins and rabbits in the snow,
Give them good faring and a warm place to go;
All little young things for His sake Who died,
Who was a Little Thing at Christmastide.

MARGARET MURRAY

Margaret W. Tarrant

Christmas

Ho! ho! thrice ho! for the mistletoe,
Ho! for the Christmas holly;
And ho! for the merry boys and girls
Who make the day so jolly.

And ho! for the deep, newfallen snow,
  For the lacework on each tree,
And ho! for the joyous Christmas bells
  That ring so merrily.

Ho! ho! thrice ho! for the fire's warm glow
  For the mirth and the cheer within;
And ho! for the tender, thoughtful hearts,
  And the children's merry din.
Ho! ho! for the strong and loving girls,
  For the manly, tender boys,
And ho! thrice ho! for the coming home
  To share in the Christmas joys.

Frank H. Sweet

So remember while December
Brings the Christmas day,
In the year let there be Christmas
In the things you do and say;
Wouldn't life be worth the living
Wouldn't dreams be coming true
If we kept the Christmas spirit
All the whole year through?

AUTHOR UNKNOWN

It is a beautiful arrangement, also, derived from days of yore, that this festival, which commemorates the announcement of the religion of peace and love, has been made the season for gathering together of family connections, and drawing closer again those bands of kindred hearts, which the cares and pleasures and sorrows of the world are continually operating to cast loose: of calling back the children of a family, who have launched forth in life, and wandered widely asunder, once more to assemble about the paternal hearth, that rallying place of the affections, there to grow young and loving again among the endearing mementos of childhood.

WASHINGTON IRVING

W hat is the Christmas spirit?

It is the spirit which brings a smile to the lips and tenderness to the heart; it is the spirit which warms one into friendship with all the world, which impels one to hold out the hand of fellowship to every man and woman.

For the Christmas motto is "Peace on earth, good-will to men," and the spirit of Christmas demands that it ring in our hearts and find expression in kindly acts and loving words.

What a joyful thing for the world it would be if the Christmas spirit could do this, not only on that holiday, but on every day of the year. What a beautiful place the world would be to live in! Peace and good-will everywhere and always! Let each one of us resolve that, so far as we are concerned, peace and good-will shall be our motto every day, and that we will do our best to make the Christmas spirit last all the year round.

AUTHOR UNKNOWN

A Christmas Wish

Many merry Christmases
Many happy New Years.

Unbroken friendships, great accumulations
of cheerful recollections
and affections on earth and heaven
for us all.

CHARLES DICKENS

A Christmas Prayer

Oh, blessed day, which givst the eternal lie
  To self and sense, and all the brute within;
Oh, come to us, amid this war of life;
  To hall and hovel come: to all who toil,
In senate, shop, or study; and to those
  Who sundered by the wastes of half a world,
Ill-warned, and sorely tempted, ever face
  Nature's brute powers, and men unmanned to brutes.
Come to them, blest and blessing, Christmas Day.
  Tell them once more the tale of Bethlehem;
The kneeling shepherds, and the Babe Divine:
  And keep them men indeed, fair Christmas Day.

CHARLES KINGSLEY

Christmas Morning

If Bethlehem were here today
Or this were very long ago,
There wouldn't be a winter time
Nor any cold or snow.

I'd run out through the garden gates,
And down along the pasture walk;
And off beside the cattle barns
I'd hear a kind of gentle talk.

I'd move the heavy iron chain
And pull away the wooden pin:
I'd push the door a little bit
And tiptoe very softly in.

The pigeons and the yellow hens
And all the cows would stand away;
Their eyes would open wide to see
A lady in the manger hay,
If this were very long ago
And Bethlehem were here today.

And Mother held my hand and smiled—
I mean the lady would—and she
Would take the woolly blankets off
Her little boy so I could see.

His shut-up eyes would be asleep,
And he would look just like our John,

And he would be all crumpled too,
And have a pinkish color on.

I'd watch his breath go in and out,
His little clothes would be all white,
I'd slip my finger in his hand
To feel how he could hold it tight.

And she would smile and say, "Take care,"
The Mother, Mary, would, "Take care";
And I would kiss his little hand
And touch his hair.

While Mary put the blankets back
The gentle talk would soon begin,
And when I'd tiptoe softly out
I'd meet the wise men going in.

ELIZABETH MADOX ROBERTS

A Lullaby for the Baby Jesus

Little Jesus, sweetly sleep, do not stir;
We will lend a coat of fur.
We will rock you, rock you, rock you,
We will rock you, rock you, rock you:

See the fur to keep you warm,
Snugly round your tiny form.
Mary's little baby, sleep, sweetly sleep,
Sleep in comfort, slumber deep;

We will rock you, rock you, rock you,
We will rock you, rock you, rock you:
We will serve you all we can,
Darling, darling little man.

CZECH CAROL

Loving Father,

help us remember the birth of Jesus,

that we may share in the song of the angels,

the gladness of the shepherds,

and the worship of the wise men.

Close the door of hate and open

the door of love all over the world.

Let kindness come with every gift

and good desires with every greeting.

Deliver us from evil by the blessing which

Christ brings, and teach us to be merry

with clear hearts.

May the Christmas morning make us happy

to be thy children,

and the Christmas evening bring us to our beds

with grateful thoughts,

forgiving and forgiven,

for Jesus' sake. Amen!

ROBERT LOUIS STEVENSON

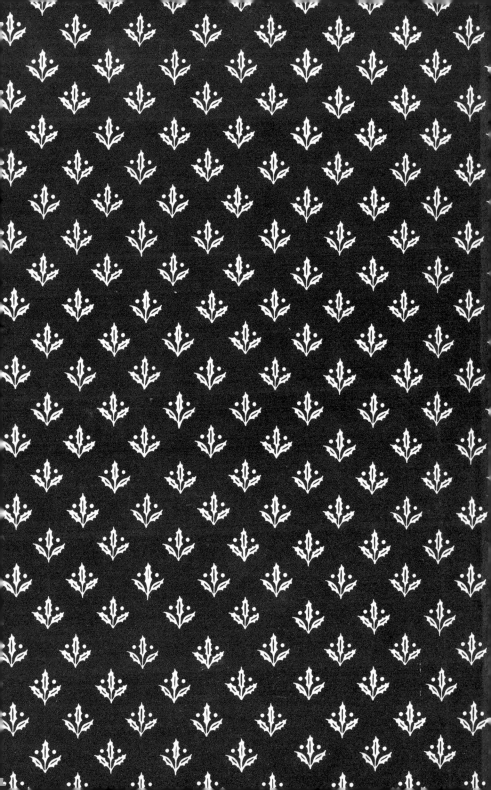